A TEACHER IS
BETTER THAN TWO BOOKS

by Linda Conway

0 43422 69502 7

Great Quotations Publishing
Glendale Heights, Illinois

1

Published in Glendale Heights, Illinois by Great Quotations Publishing.

Great Quotations
1967 Quincy Court
Glendale Heights, Il 60139
ISBN 1-56245-055-7

Printed in Hong Kong

This book is dedicated to
all who guide and influence the
minds and souls of others and to
all of my students who have taught me
some of life's more important lessons.

IT IS NOT THE I.Q.
BUT THE I WILL THAT IS
IMPORTANT IN EDUCATION.

MY DAILY LESSON PLAN:

TODAY I WILL TEACH THE IMPORTANCE OF DEDICATED EFFORT AND PERSEVERENCE.

FIRST GRADE TEACHER:
ONE WHO KNOWS HOW TO
MAKE LITTLE THINGS COUNT.

MY DAILY LESSON PLAN:

TODAY I WILL REMEMBER TO COMPLIMENT, ENCOURAGE, AND MONITOR THE PROGRESS OF OTHERS.

IT'S NOT WHAT IS POURED
INTO A STUDENT THAT
COUNTS, BUT WHAT IS
PLANTED.

MY DAILY LESSON PLAN:

TODAY I WILL "PLANT" WHAT IS RELEVANT, SUSTAINING, ENRICHING AND TRUE!

A TEACHER AFFECTS
ETERNITY; HE CAN NEVER TELL
WHERE HIS INFLUENCE STOPS.

- HENRY BROOKS ADAMS

MY DAILY LESSON PLAN:

TODAY I WILL BE A POSITIVE INFLUENCE AND MY CLASSROOM A POSITIVE ENVIRONMENT FOR MY STUDENTS.

SIXTY YEARS AGO I KNEW
EVERYTHING; NOW I KNOW
NOTHING; EDUCATION IS A
PROGRESSIVE DISCOVERY OF
OUR OWN IGNORANCE.

- WILL DURANT

MY DAILY LESSON PLAN:

TODAY I WILL REALIZE HOW LITTLE I KNOW.

AS IMPORTANT AS
'HANGING ON' IS KNOWING
WHEN TO 'LET GO.'

MY DAILY LESSON PLAN:

TODAY I WILL REALIZE MY PERSONAL AND PROFESSIONAL LIMITS.

TO BE ABLE TO BE CAUGHT UP
INTO THE WORLD OF THOUGHT
— THAT IS BEING EDUCATED.

- EDITH HAMILTON

MY DAILY LESSON PLAN:

TODAY I WILL BE THANKFUL FOR HEALTHY, ACTIVE MINDS.

A TEACHER IS BETTER THAN TWO BOOKS.

EDUCATION TODAY, MORE THAN EVER BEFORE, MUST SEE CLEARLY THE DUAL OBJECTIVES: EDUCATION FOR LIVING AND EDUCATING FOR MAKING A LIVING.

- JAMES MASON WOOD

MY DAILY LESSON PLAN:

TODAY I WILL BE CONSCIOUS OF THE GREATER SCHEME OF THINGS AND RELATIVE IMPORTANCE OF MY CONTRIBUTION TO IT.

IF THERE IS ANYTHING EDUCATION DOES NOT LACK TODAY, IT IS CRITICS.

- NATHAN M. PUSEY

MY DAILY LESSON PLAN:

TODAY I WILL MAKE A SPECIAL EFFORT TO ELIMINATE CRITICAL COMMENTS.

THE LEAST EXPENSIVE
EDUCATION IS TO PROFIT
FROM THE MISTAKES OF
OTHERS — AND OURSELVES.

MY DAILY LESSON PLAN:

TODAY I WILL REMIND MYSELF AND OTHERS THAT MISTAKES ARE LESSONS TOO.

THE SECRET OF EDUCATION IS RESPECTING THE PUPIL.

- RALPH W. EMERSON

MY DAILY LESSON PLAN:

TODAY I WILL SHOW OTHERS THE RESPECT I WISH TO BE SHOWN.

IF IN INSTRUCTING A CHILD, YOU ARE VEXED WITH IT FOR WANT OF ADROITNESS, TRY, IF YOU HAVE NEVER TRIED BEFORE, TO WRITE WITH YOUR LEFT HAND, AND THEN REMEMBER THAT A CHILD IS ALL LEFT HAND.

- J.F. BOYSE, *TALES FROM HOFFMAN*

MY DAILY LESSON PLAN:

TODAY I WILL BE ESPECIALLY AWARE AND SUPPORTIVE OF ALL THOSE WHO STRUGGLE TO SUCCEED.

THE TRAINING OF CHILDREN IS A PROFESSION, WHERE WE MUST KNOW HOW TO WASTE TIME IN ORDER TO SAVE IT.

- JEAN JACQUES ROUSSEAU

MY DAILY LESSON PLAN:

TODAY I WILL "WASTE" TIME WISELY AND FOR THE ENRICHMENT OF ALL - MYSELF INCLUDED!

A CHILD'S EDUCATION SHOULD BEGIN AT LEAST ONE HUNDRED YEARS BEFORE HE IS BORN.

- OLIVER W. HOLMES

MY DAILY LESSON PLAN:

TODAY I RECOGNIZE THAT I GET TO CARRY THIS TORCH FOR ONE BRIEF MOMENT IN TIME.

THERE IS NOTHING SO
UNEQUAL AS THE EQUAL
TREATMENT OF UNEQUALS.
INDIVIDUALIZE YOUR
LEADERSHIP.

MY DAILY LESSON PLAN:

TODAY I WILL TEACH WITH A VITALITY THAT IS UNIQUELY "ME," RECOGNIZING EACH STUDENTS' SIMILAR RIGHT.

I HAVE OFTEN THOUGHT WHAT A MELANCHOLY WORLD THIS WOULD BE WITHOUT CHILDREN, AND WHAT AN INHUMAN WORLD WITHOUT THE AGED.

- SAMUEL T. COLERIDGE

MY DAILY LESSON PLAN:

TODAY I WILL ENJOY MY STUDENTS' IMMATURITY - THEIR NATURAL BIRTHRIGHT - REMEMBERING I, TOO, AM STILL IMMATURE (BY MY PARENTS' STANDARDS)!

FOUR-YEAR-OLD'S DEFINITION OF NURSERY SCHOOL: A PLACE WHERE THEY TRY TO TEACH CHILDREN WHO HIT, NOT TO HIT, AND CHILDREN WHO DON'T HIT, TO HIT BACK.

- MRS. M.S.N., *PARENTS' MAGAZINE*

MY DAILY LESSON PLAN:

TODAY I REALIZE LESSONS TAKE AN INFINITE VARIETY OF FORM.

LET US ALWAYS BE OPEN TO
THE MIRACLE OF THE SECOND
CHANCE.

- REV. DAVID STIER

MY DAILY LESSON PLAN:

TODAY I WILL REMEMBER ALL THE TIMES I NEEDED A SECOND CHANCE AND SOMEONE GAVE IT TO ME. LET ME BE SO GENEROUS.

REASONING WITH A CHILD IS FINE, IF YOU CAN REACH THE CHILD'S REASON WITHOUT DESTROYING YOUR OWN.

- JOHN MASON BROWN

MY DAILY LESSON PLAN:

TODAY I WILL REMAIN IN CONTROL OF MY THOUGHTS AND ACTIONS REGARDLESS OF CIRCUMSTANCE.

WE SHOULDN'T TEACH GREAT BOOKS, WE SHOULD TEACH A LOVE OF READING.

- B.F. SKINNER

MY DAILY LESSON PLAN:

TODAY I WILL READ AND SPEAK WITH A PASSION AND EXPRESSION THAT SHALL MAKE THEM FEEL THE VIBRATION OF LIFE ITSELF.

READING IS TO THE MIND
THAT EXERCISE IS TO THE
BODY.

- RICHARD STEELE, *THE TATLER, NO. 147*

MY DAILY LESSON PLAN:

TODAY I WILL EXERCISE MY MIND, BODY, AND SPIRIT — NOURISHMENT FOR LIFE.

SETTING AN EXAMPLE IS NOT THE MAIN MEANS OF INFLUENCING ANOTHER, IT IS THE ONLY MEANS.

- ALBERT EINSTEIN

MY DAILY LESSON PLAN:

TODAY I WILL REMEMBER
THE POWER OF EXAMPLE AND
TRY TO BE THE BEST EXAMPLE
I KNOW HOW TO BE FOR
OTHERS.

THE YOUNG ARE PERMANENTLY IN A STATE RESEMBLING INTOXICATION; FOR YOUTH IS SWEET AND THEY ARE GROWING.

- ARISTOTLE

MY DAILY LESSON PLAN:

TODAY I WILL DELIGHT IN
THE ENERGIES, CREATIVITY,
RESPONSIVENESS AND
SPONTANEITY OF ALL WHO I
ENCOUNTER. I WILL PASS NO
JUDGEMENT.

THE DREAM BEGINS WITH A TEACHER WHO BELIEVES IN YOU, WHO TUGS AND PUSHES AND LEADS YOU TO THE NEXT PLATEAU, SOMETIMES POKING YOU WITH A SHARP STICK CALLED "TRUTH."

- DAN RATHER

MY DAILY LESSON PLAN:

TODAY I WILL BE ESPECIALLY AWARE OF THOSE WHO NEED A LOVING PUSH, A GENTLE TUG, OR A GUIDING HAND.

AT THE DESK WHERE I SIT, I HAVE LEARNED ONE GREAT TRUTH. THE ANSWER FOR ALL OUR NATIONAL PROBLEMS — THE ANSWER FOR ALL THE PROBLEMS OF THE WORLD — COMES TO A SINGLE WORD. THAT WORD IS "EDUCATION."

- LYNDON B. JOHNSON

MY DAILY LESSON PLAN:

TODAY I WILL REALIZE THAT WHAT I DO IS IMPORTANT!

A SCHOOL SHOULD NOT BE A PREPARATION FOR LIFE. A SCHOOL SHOULD BE LIFE.

- ELBERT HUBBARD

MY DAILY LESSON PLAN:

TODAY I WILL CREATE A LABORATORY FOR LIFE IN MY CLASSROOM.

WE'LL BE IN TROUBLE AS LONG AS WE PAY THE BEST PROFESSORS LESS THAN THE WORST FOOTBALL COACH.

MY DAILY LESSON PLAN:

TODAY I WILL DO MY PART
TO SUPPORT PROFESSIONAL
ORGANIZATIONS AND KEEP
FOCUS ON THE PRIMARY
GOALS OF EDUCATION —
DESPITE PUBLIC PRESSURE
AND OPINION.

AS A GENERAL RULE,
TEACHERS TEACH MORE BY
WHAT THEY ARE THAN BY
WHAT THEY SAY.

MY DAILY LESSON PLAN:

TODAY I UNDERSTAND THAT MY ACTIONS WILL DOUBTLESS SPEAK LOUDER THAN MY WORDS — MAY THEY BE NOBLE.

EDUCATION MAKES PEOPLE
EASY TO LEAD BUT DIFFICULT
TO DRIVE; EASY TO GOVERN
BUT IMPOSSIBLE TO ENSLAVE.

MY DAILY LESSON PLAN:

TODAY I WILL ADVISE OTHERS THAT EDUCATION AIDS CIVILIZATIONS TO MAKE HEALTHIER CHOICES.

MATHEMATICS IS THE DOOR AND THE KEY TO THE SCIENCES.

- ROGER BACON

MY DAILY LESSON PLAN:

TODAY I WILL ENCOURAGE MY STUDENTS TO BUILD THE STRONGEST FOUNDATION THEY CAN.

LITERATURE IS MY UTOPIA.

- HELLEN KELLER

A TEACHER IS BETTER THAN TWO BOOKS.

MY DAILY LESSON PLAN:

TODAY I WILL RECOGNIZE
THAT ALL GREAT LITERATURE
IS TIMELESS AND UNIVERSAL
AS IT SPEAKS OF LIFE'S
TRUTHS.

EDUCATION CAN'T MAKE US ALL LEADERS — BUT IT CAN TEACH US WHICH LEADER TO FOLLOW.

MY DAILY LESSON PLAN:

TODAY I WILL REMIND OTHERS THAT INTELLIGENT PEOPLE CAN MAKE MORE INTELLIGENT DECISIONS.

FLOWERS LEAVE PART OF THEIR FRAGRANCE IN THE HANDS THAT BESTOW THEM.

- CHINESE PROVERB

MY DAILY LESSON PLAN:

TODAY I WILL GIVE "FLOWERS" FREELY AND UNCONDITIONALLY.

NO ONE LIKE YOU WAS EVER BORN OR EVER WILL BE.

- CONSTANCE FOSTER

MY DAILY LESSON PLAN:

TODAY I RESPECT MY INDIVIDUALITY AND THAT OF OTHERS.

EFFICIENT SCHOOL TEACHERS MAY COST MORE, BUT POOR SCHOOL TEACHERS COST THE MOST.

MY DAILY LESSON PLAN:

TODAY I WILL ENCOURAGE PROSPECTIVE AND BEGINNING TEACHERS, OFFERING SUPPORT AND COUNSEL.

ONE REASON FOR JUVENILE DELINQUENCY IS THAT MANY PARENTS ARE RAISING THEIR CHILDREN BY REMOTE CONTROL.

MY DAILY LESSON PLAN:

TODAY I ACKNOWLEDGE A CERTAIN LACK OF PARENTAL AND PERSONAL DISCIPLINE AND INVOLVEMENT, AND HOPE MY EFFORTS ADDRESS THESE DEFICIENCIES.

ALL OF US HAVE TWO EDUCATIONS; ONE WHICH WE RECEIVE FROM OTHERS; ANOTHER, AND THE MOST VALUABLE, WHICH WE GIVE OURSELVES.

- JOHN RANDOLPH

A TEACHER IS BETTER THAN TWO BOOKS.

MY DAILY LESSON PLAN:

TODAY I WILL REMEMBER
THAT I SPEND EVERY DAY
BEING A STUDENT (OF LIFE).

CONVERSATION IS THE LABORATORY AND WORKSHOP OF THE STUDENT.

- RALPH WALDO EMERSON

MY DAILY LESSON PLAN:

TODAY I WILL VALUE CONVERSATIONS WITH MY STUDENTS, LISTENING ATTENTIVELY TO EVERY WORD.

A PRIME FUNCTION OF A LEADER IS TO KEEP HOPE ALIVE.

- JOHN W. GARDNER

MY DAILY LESSON PLAN:

TODAY I WILL NURTURE HOPE IN MY CLASSROOM.

FORMULA FOR TACT: BE BRIEF, POLITELY; BE AGGRESSIVE, SMILINGLY; BE EMPHATIC, PLEASANTLY; BE POSITIVE, DIPLOMATICALLY; BE RIGHT, GRACIOUSLY.

MY DAILY LESSON PLAN:

TODAY I WILL PRACTICE THE FORMULA FOR TACT.

Don't be a carbon copy of something. Make your own impressions.

MY DAILY LESSON PLAN:

TODAY I WILL EMBELLISH ALL I DO WITH MY PERSONAL, CREATIVE IMPRESSION.

WE TRY TO SEE SOME GOOD IN EVERYBODY WE MEET, BUT OCCASIONALLY THERE ARE SOME FOLKS WHO MAKE US REALIZE OUR EYESIGHT ISN'T AS GOOD AS IT ONCE WAS.

MY DAILY LESSON PLAN:

TODAY I WILL MAKE EVERY
ATTEMPT TO SEE THE GOOD IN
ALL THAT I ENCOUNTER.

TO REALLY KNOW A MAN, OBSERVE HIS BEHAVIOR WITH A WOMAN, A FLAT TIRE, AND A CHILD.

MY DAILY LESSON PLAN:

TODAY I WILL PUT FORTH
AN EFFORT TO OBSERVE MY
STUDENTS IN OTHER SETTINGS
(LUNCH, HALLS, ACTIVITIES).

SOME PARENTS BRING THEIR CHILDREN UP, OTHERS LET THEM DOWN.

MY DAILY LESSON PLAN:

TODAY I SADLY ADMIT THAT SOME OF MY STUDENTS AND FRIENDS HAVE BEEN "PARENTALLY ABANDONED" THROUGH NO FAULT OF THEIR OWN.

SCHOOL TEACHERS ARE GIVEN TOO MUCH CREDIT AND TOO LITTLE CASH.

MY DAILY LESSON PLAN:

TODAY I WILL SUPPORT
EFFORTS TO ENHANCE MY
PROFESSION SO THAT THE
FUTURE FOR TEACHERS IS
PROMISING AND ATTRACTIVE.

THE FUNCTION OF WISDOM IS DISCRIMINATING BETWEEN GOOD AND EVIL.

- CICERO

MY DAILY LESSON PLAN:

TODAY I WILL MAKE HEALTHY DECISIONS FOR MYSELF AND ENCOURAGE MY STUDENTS TO DO LIKEWISE.

YOUTH IS EASILY DECEIVED BECAUSE IT IS QUICK TO HOPE.

- ARISTOTLE

MY DAILY LESSON PLAN:

TODAY I WILL RECOGNIZE THE IMPRESSIONABILITY OF THE YOUNG MINDS I TEACH. LET MY WORDS, THOUGHTS AND DEEDS BE POSITIVE, ENRICHING IMPRESSIONS.

MEN LOVE TO WONDER, AND THAT IS THE SEED OF SCIENCE.

- RALPH WALDO EMERSON

MY DAILY LESSON PLAN:

TODAY I WILL NURTURE THE SENSE OF WONDER IN MYSELF AND MY STUDENTS.

THE MATHEMATICIAN HAS REACHED THE HIGHEST RUNG ON THE LADDER OF HUMAN THOUGHT.

- HAVELOCK ELLIS

MY DAILY LESSON PLAN:

TODAY I ADMIRE THE ABILITIES OF THOSE WHOSE MINDS THINK IN PRAGMATIC WAYS.

ANGELS CAN FLY BECAUSE
THEY TAKE THEMSELVES
LIGHTLY.

- G.K. CHESTERTON

MY DAILY LESSON PLAN:

TODAY I WILL ENCOURAGE MY STUDENTS TO FLY - TO NOT TAKE THEMSELVES TOO SERIOUSLY.

THERE IS ONLY ONE CORNER
OF THE UNIVERSE YOU CAN BE
CERTAIN OF IMPROVING, AND
THAT'S YOUR OWN SELF.

- ALDOUS HUXLEY

MY DAILY LESSON PLAN:

TODAY I WILL REAFFIRM THE FACT THAT I AM A STUDENT OF THE UNIVERSE.

THERE IS A CHARM ABOUT THE FORBIDDEN THAT MAKES IT UNSPEAKABLY DESIRABLE.

- MARK TWAIN, *NOTEBOOKS*

MY DAILY LESSON PLAN:

TODAY I RECOGNIZE THE POWER OF THE FORBIDDEN AND WILL GENTLY REDIRECT FOCUS AND ENERGY.

COME WHAT MAY, TIME AND THE HOUR RUNS THROUGH THE ROUGHEST DAY.

- SHAKESPEARE, *MACBETH I, III*

MY DAILY LESSON PLAN:

TODAY I AM AWARE THAT TIME IS RELENTLESS AND CONSTANT - CURSE OR A BLESSING??

THE HIGHEST RESULT OF EDUCATION IS TOLERANCE.

- HELEN KELLER *OPTIMISM*

MY DAILY LESSON PLAN:

TODAY I WILL EXERCISE TOLERANCE AND ENCOURAGE OTHERS TO ALSO.

EVERY PERSON'S FEELINGS HAVE A FRONT-DOOR AND A SIDE-DOOR BY WHICH THEY MAY BE ENTERED.

- OLIVER WENDELL HOLMES

MY DAILY LESSON PLAN:

TODAY I WILL CHALLENGE MYSELF AND OTHERS TO PURSUE PERSONAL GOALS ONE STEP AT A TIME.

COMING TOGETHER IS A
BEGINNING; KEEPING
TOGETHER IS PROGRESS;
WORKING TOGETHER IS
SUCCESS.

- HENRY FORD

MY DAILY LESSON PLAN:

TODAY I WILL ENCOURAGE TEAMWORK WITH OTHERS AND BE A PRODUCTIVE TEAM MEMBER MYSELF.

I KNOW OF NO GREAT MAN
EXCEPT THOSE WHO HAVE
RENDERED GREAT SERVICES
TO THE HUMAN RACE.

VOLTAIRE

A TEACHER IS BETTER THAN TWO BOOKS.

MY DAILY LESSON PLAN:

TODAY I WILL REALIZE GREATNESS ALL AROUND ME.

Other Titles By Great Quotations

201 Best Things Ever Said
The ABC's of Parenting
As a Cat Thinketh
The Best of Friends
The Birthday Astrologer
Chicken Soup & Other Yiddish Say
Cornerstones of Success
Don't Deliberate ... Litigate!
Fantastic Father, Dependable Dad
Global Wisdom
Golden Years, Golden Words
Grandma, I Love You
Growing up in Toyland
Happiness is Found Along The Way
Hollywords
Hooked on Golf
In Celebration of Women
Inspirations Compelling Food for Thought
I'm Not Over the Hill
Let's Talk Decorating
Life's Lessons
Life's Simple Pleasures
A Light Heart Lives Long
Money for Nothing, Tips for Free

Mother, I Love You
Motivating Quotes for Motivated People
Mrs. Aesop's Fables
Mrs. Murphy's Laws
Mrs. Webster's Dictionary
My Daughter, My Special Friend
Other Species
Parenting 101
Reflections
Romantic Rhapsody
The Secret Language of Men
The Secret Language of Women
Some Things Never Change
The Sports Page
Sports Widow
Stress or Sanity
Teacher is Better than Two Books
Teenage of Insanity
Thanks from the Heart
Things You'll Learn if You Live Long Enough
Wedding Wonders
Working Women's World
Interior Design for Idiots
Dear Mr. President

GREAT QUOTATIONS PUBLISHING COMPANY
1967 Quincy Court
Glendale Heights, IL 60139 - 2045
Phone (630) 582-2800
Fax (630) 582- 2813